CLAWS AND PAWS

Martha K. Resnick

Carolyn J. Hyatt

STECK-VAUGHN
ELEMENTARY · SECONDARY · ADULT · LIBRARY

A Harcourt Company

www.steck-vaughn.com

About the Authors

MARTHA K. RESNICK is an experienced elementary teacher, formerly a Reading Resource Teacher with the Baltimore City Schools. She has served as a cooperative practice teacher, training student teachers from many colleges. Mrs. Resnick received her master's degree in education at Loyola College.

CAROLYN J. HYATT has taught elementary, secondary, and adult education classes. She was formerly a Senior Teacher with the Baltimore City Schools. Mrs. Hyatt received her master's degree in education at Loyola College.

Reading Comprehension Series

Wags & Tags

Claws & Paws

Gills & Bills

Manes & Reins

Bones & Stones

Swells & Shells

Heights & Flights

Trails & Dales

Acknowledgments

Illustrated by Rosemarie Fox-Hicks, Sue Durban, and David Cunningham

Cover design Linda Adkins Design

Cover photograph © Superstock

All photographs used with permission. Interior photographs: © 1988 E. R. Degginger/ Hillstrom Stock Photo; © 1988 Graphic Masters Inc./David Roth; © 1988 Kenji Kerins

ISBN 0-8114-1341-1

Contents

This animal has a big tail.
It has big back paws.
It jumps on its back feet.
Its front paws are like hands.

Look at your little finger.
This animal's new baby is that little.
The baby has no fur. It can not see.
It lives in the mother's pouch.
It lives there a long time.
It gets big in the pouch.
What animal is this?

A **Which one is right? Put a ✔ by it.**
One is done for you.

1. What has a pouch?

   _____ a. a new baby

   _____ b. your hand

   _✔_ c. the mother animal

2. What animal is this?

   _____ a. kangaroo

   _____ b. rabbit

   _____ c. lion

3. Where must a new baby kangaroo live?

   _____ a. in an egg

   _____ b. in the mother's pouch

   _____ c. in a nest

4. How do these animals walk?

   _____ a. on four paws

   _____ b. on three paws

   _____ c. on two paws

5. What is a good name for this story?

   _____ a. A Little Finger

   _____ b. A Funny Animal

   _____ c. A Little Bunny

6. What do you know about the new baby?

_____ a. It has brown fur.

_____ b. It has no back paws.

_____ c. It can not see.

B **Draw lines to match the words.**
One is done for you.

1. a bag

2. not old

3. to jump

4. not the front

5. It is on your hand.

6. an animal's feet

paws

talk

pouch

hop

finger

new

back

C **Write the words in the right place.**
One is done for you.

paw	pouch	fur	tail
hop	back	front	

1. fur

2. _____

3. _____

4. _____

5. _____

6. _____

1. Kangaroos are funny animals.

She
(They)	jump far.

2. The new baby can not see.

It
They	can not jump.

3. The mother kangaroo has a pouch.

He
She	has a baby in the pouch.

4. The kangaroo's <u>tail</u> is big.

She
It	is not little.

5. Father kangaroo lives far away.

He
She	can hop fast.

6. Baby kangaroos have no fur.

It
They	will get fur soon.

7. The pouch is on the kangaroo.

It
They	has a baby in it.

"Bath time!" said Jill.
Tags said to Wags, "Oh, oh, time to run away!"
Wags said, "No bath for me!"
But Jill and Dan were too fast.
Into the bath tub went Wags.
Into the tub went Tags.
They got a good bath.
Dan said, "The dogs look good now."

In the morning the dogs ran out to play.
They saw a big mud puddle.
In they jumped.

"Now this is fun," said the little animals.

A **Which one is right? Put a ✔ by it.**

1. Who got a bath?

_____ a. Dan

_____ b. animals

_____ c. Jill

8

2. Where did they get a bath?

_____ a. in a bed

_____ b. in a tub

_____ c. in some mud

3. When did the dogs go out to play?

_____ a. at night

_____ b. at one o'clock

_____ c. in the morning

4. Why did the children put the dogs into the bath tub?

_____ a. The dogs wanted a bath.

_____ b. The children wanted a bath.

_____ c. The children wanted the dogs to look good.

5. What do you think happened to the dogs after they played in the mud?

_____ a. The children said, "Good dogs!"

_____ b. The dogs went into the tub again.

_____ c. Jill and Dan jumped in the mud.

6. What is a good name for this story?

_____ a. The Big Bath Tub

_____ b. Two Dogs in a Tub

_____ c. A Little Puddle

B Draw lines to match these.

1. It is brown and black.

2. Where the dogs got a bath

3. It is a time.

4. They walked away.

5. Tags has one.

6. It is not the front.

7. It is a good time.

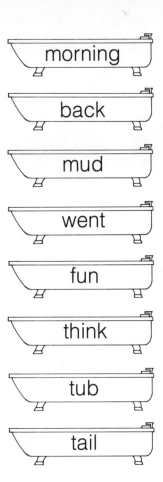

morning

back

mud

went

fun

think

tub

tail

C Read each sentence. Finish it.
Circle the right picture.

1. It is time for the dogs to eat. Wags went to _____ .
   a.   b.    c.

2. Dan gets out of bed. He will get into the _____ .
   a.   b.   c.

3. This is on your hand. It is your _____ .
   a.    b.    c.

D WHO? WHAT? Circle the right word for each story.

1. Jill saw the mud.

   Jill did not like | them / it | .

2. Dan ran to the dogs.

   He went to | they / them | .

3. The puddles are by the flowers.

   | They / It | have water in them.

4. I see the bath tub.

   It has water in | them / it | .

5. Jill is not home.

   | He / She | is not here.

E Can you tell the story? Some things are not in the right place. Put **1, 2,** and **3** in the boxes. One is done for you.

| 1 | The dogs went into the tub.

| | The dogs played in the mud.

| | Dan said, "The dogs look good."

11

3 One day Mother Duck walked.
She walked on the grass.

She said, "Let's swim in the water.
You will do something new.
Do what I do.
It will be fun."

The ducks have food.
They got it in the pond.
The little ducks did something new.

A Which one is right? Put a ✔ by it.
One is done for you.

1. When did this story happen?

   ✔ a. day

   ____ b. night

   ____ c. at the pond

2. Where did Mother take the baby ducks?

   ____ a. to the farm

   ____ b. to the water

   ____ c. to school

3. What new thing did the baby ducks do?

   ____ a. get food

   ____ b. go to sleep

   ____ c. play a game

4. How do baby ducks learn?

   ____ a. by reading a book

   ____ b. by eating fish

   ____ c. by looking at big ducks

5. What is the best name for this story?

   ____ a. Baby Ducks Can Fly

   ____ b. Baby Ducks Run Away

   ____ c. Baby Ducks Do Something New

B Draw lines to match the words.
One is done for you.

food

fun

pond

1. not old

new

2. something to eat

3. to go fast in the water

do

4. some water

5. a good time

walk

6. something feet can do

swim

C Each picture goes with a sentence.
Draw lines to match them.

a.

1. Flowers are in the pond.

2. A duck is flying.

b.

3. Ducks swim.

4. The ducks walk with Mother.

c.

5. A duck is eating.

14

d.

D **WHO?**
WHAT?   Circle the right word. One is done for you.

1. The ducks are on the grass.

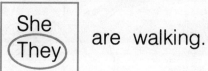

are walking.

2. The flower was in the pond.

It
He

was white.

3. Fish can swim.

We
They

can go fast.

4. Ann is by the water.

He
She

looks at the fish.

5. Tim can swim.

He
They

can have fun.

E Can you tell the story? Some things are not in
the right place. Put **1**, **2**, and **3** in the boxes.
One is done for you.

[ ] The ducks went into the water.

[ ] They got food.

[1] The ducks walked on the grass.

4

One morning the robins were working.
They were making a nest.
The nest was in an old oak tree.
Mr. Robin found some grass for the nest.
Mrs. Robin got mud for the nest.
The nest was made of mud and grass.
Soon Mrs. Robin will lay eggs in the nest.
The eggs will be blue.
What will come out of the robins' eggs?

A **Which one is right? Put a ✔ by it.**

1. When were the robins working?

_____ a. at night

_____ b. at noon

_____ c. in the morning

2. What were the robins making?

_____ a. a school

_____ b. a home

_____ c. an oak tree

16

3. Where was the nest?

_____ a. in an apple tree

_____ b. in the brown sand

_____ c. in an oak tree

4. What was used to make the nest?

_____ a. grass and mud

_____ b. sand and mud

_____ c. grass and sand

5. What will Mrs. Robin do?

_____ a. dig a hole

_____ b. lay eggs in the nest

_____ c. play and run

6. What color is a robin's egg?

_____ a. white _____ b. brown _____ c. blue

7. What will come out of robins' eggs?

_____ a. baby chickens

_____ b. baby birds

_____ c. baby turtles

8. What is the best name for the story?

_____ a. A Nest in the Sand

_____ b. A Nest in a Tree

_____ c. A Nest in the Grass

B **Draw lines to match these. One is done for you.**

1. green plants

2. time of the day

3. kind of bird

4. what a woman is called

5. a tree

6. color of a robin's egg

7. what a man is called

8. home for birds

robin

morning

Mrs.

grass

oak

Mr.

nest

blue

make

C **Each picture goes with a sentence.**
Draw lines to match them.

1. The robin finds some grass.

2. Three eggs are in the nest.

3. The robins make a nest.

4. The oak tree is big.

5. Two eggs are in the nest.

a.

b.

c.

d.

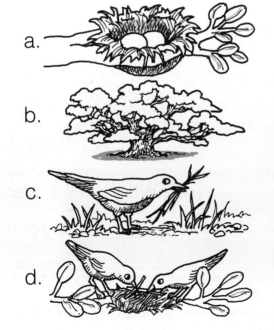

D WHO?
WHAT? **Circle the right word for each story.**

1. The eggs are blue.

   What will come out of | them
   it | ?

2. Mr. Robin and Mrs. Robin made a nest.

   | They
   She | got grass for the nest.

3. Mrs. Robin saw a man.

   Mrs. Robin went away from | them
   him | .

4. The birds live in the tree.

   They have a nest in | it
   them | .

5. Mrs. Robin will lay eggs soon.

   | Our
   Her | eggs will be blue.

E **Can you tell the story? Some things are not in the right place. Put 1, 2, and 3 in the boxes. One is done for you.**

☐ Mrs. Robin will lay eggs in the nest.

☐ They made a nest in the oak tree.

1 Mr. and Mrs. Robin got grass and mud.

5

One afternoon Mom wanted some food. Ann and Andy went to the store for her. They walked a long way down Duck Street. Then they went around a corner. They walked by the park. Then they got to the store.

Ann and Andy found eggs, bread, fish, and milk. A woman put the food into a bag for them. They gave the woman some money. Then Ann and Andy walked home.

When Mom looked inside the bag, she said, "You forgot the lettuce!"

Ann and Andy had to go all the way back to the store. Then they had to walk home again.

A **Which one is right? Put a ✔ by it.**

1. Who went to the store?

_____ a. two children

_____ b. Mom

_____ c. two boys

2. When did they go to the store?

_____ a. at night

_____ b. in the morning

_____ c. in the afternoon

3. Where did the woman put the food?

_____ a. in a bag

_____ b. in a box

_____ c. in the park

4. What did Ann and Andy give the woman?

_____ a. food _____ b. lettuce _____ c. money

5. Why did Ann and Andy go back to the store?

_____ a. to get money

_____ b. to get lettuce

_____ c. to see Mom there

6. What do we know about the store?

_____ a. It was a long way from home.

_____ b. It was next to Ann and Andy's house.

_____ c. It was on Old Street.

7. What is the best name for this story?

_____ a. The Lost Lettuce

_____ b. Fun at the Store

_____ c. Two Long Walks

B **Draw lines to match these. One is done for you.**

1. a place to play

2. did not think about

3. a green food

4. a white drink

5. We pay with it.

6. boys and girls

7. a time of day

8. where two streets
come together

lettuce

milk

park

forgot

corner

duck

afternoon

children

money

C **Pick out the right word from the bag.**
Write the word. One is done for you.

walk   black   milk
day   house   girl

1. lettuce, bread, eggs,   milk

2. school, store, home,

3. run, skip, jump,

4. Mom, woman, sister,

5. green, blue, brown,

D WHO? WHAT? **Circle the right word for each story.**

1. The lettuce was green.

It	
They	was in a brown bag.

2. Ann got some eggs.

   She wanted to eat | it |
   | them | .

3. The children went down Duck Street.

She	
They	went around the corner.

4. Andy had some money.

He	
She	gave it to a woman.

5. Ann walked with Andy.

   Ann was next to | her |
   | him | .

E Can you tell the story? Some things are not in the right place. Put **1, 2,** and **3** in the boxes.

☐ Ann and Andy forgot to get the lettuce.

☐ Mother wanted some food from the store.

☐ Ann and Andy had to go back to the store.

A Read the question. Write the answers next to each one. How many paws do they have? Write the words.

zero   one   four

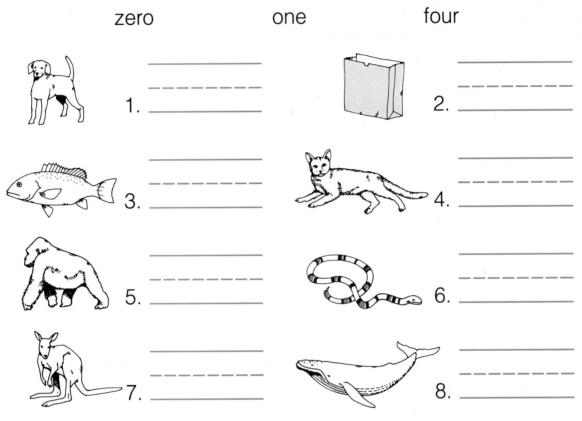

1. _____

2. _____

3. _____

4. _____

5. _____

6. _____

7. _____

8. _____

B WHO? WHAT? Circle the right word for each story.

1. Dad got some eggs at the store.

   | He |
   | She | took the eggs home.

2. Mom forgot to take the bags.

   She had to go home to get | it |
                              | them | .

3. Ann and Andy ran around the corner.

   | They |
   | She | ran fast.

C **Draw lines to match these.**

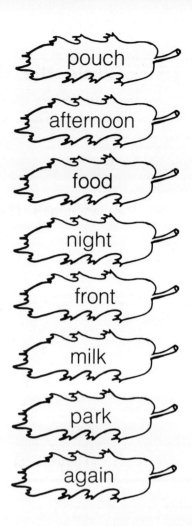

pouch

afternoon

food

night

front

milk

park

again

1. a kind of bag

2. something to eat

3. time after morning

4. one more time

5. place to play

6. time for bed

7. not the back

D **Read each sentence. Finish it.**
Circle the right picture.

1. Mrs. Robin will lay a blue ____ in the nest.

a.　　　　　　　　　b.　　　　　　　　　c.

2. The kangaroo has a big ____ .

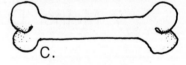

a.　　　　　　　　　b.　　　　　　　　　c.

3. The little ducks eat ____.

a.　　　　　　　　　b.　　　　　　　　　c.

E **Circle the right word.**

1. We saw the kangaroo [hot / hop] in the tall grass.

2. Robins make a nest of [grass / green] and [mad / mud] .

3. Wags and Tags had a bath in a [but / tub] .

4. Ann and Andy [forgot / four] the lettuce.

5. They had to go [black / back] to the store.

6. Mother gave them [money / many] to get food.

7. Mother Duck walked on the [goats / grass] .

F **Can you tell about Story 5? Some things are not in the right place. Put 1, 2, and 3 in the boxes.**

[   ] A woman put the food into a bag.

[   ] Mom said, "You forgot the lettuce!"

[   ] Ann and Andy walked to the store.

26

Each picture goes with a sentence.
Draw lines to match them.

1.
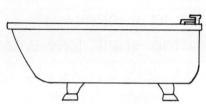

a. The baby gets big
   in the pouch.

2.

b. People can get a bath
   in this tub.

3.

c. Tags lives in this
   dog house.

d. The robins look for
   food.

4.

e. The children got
   them at the store.

5

f. The robins made a
   nest of grass and
   mud.

6

Mom and Dad wanted the children to take care of their toys. Every night the children put all the big toys in their rooms. Then they put all the little toys on a toy shelf. Each child had a shelf.

Bob was ten. He had the top shelf. Bev was eight. She had the middle shelf. Bill was seven. He had the bottom shelf.

On Sunday evening, Dad and Mom found lots of toys on the rug. They went to look at the toy shelf. They saw no toys on the middle shelf.

Mom said, "Now I know who did not put the toys away."

Dad said, "I can guess who it is, too."

Can you guess who forgot to put away toys?

A **Which one is right? Put a ✓ by it.**

1. What was the story about?

_____ a. getting a new rug

_____ b. getting a toy shelf

_____ c. a child who forgot to do something

28

2. What did Mom and Dad want the children to do?

_____ a. go to the store

_____ b. put away the toys

_____ c. make a new shelf

3. Where did the children put their big toys?

_____ a. on a shelf

_____ b. under a bed

_____ c. in their rooms

4. Where did Dad and Mom find some toys?

_____ a. on the chair

_____ b. on the rug

_____ c. at the store

5. When did Dad and Mom find toys on the rug?

_____ a. Tuesday evening

_____ b. Sunday evening

_____ c. Sunday afternoon

6. Who forgot to put the toys away?

_____ a. Bev   _____ b. Bill   _____ c. Bob

7. How did Mom know who did not put away toys?

_____ a. She saw toys on every shelf.

_____ b. She saw no toys on one shelf.

_____ c. She asked the children.

B **Draw lines to match these.**

1. six and one

2. part that is under

3. day of the week

4. late in the day

5. seven and one

6. place to put things on

7. all of them

8. things to play with

9. not the top or
   the bottom

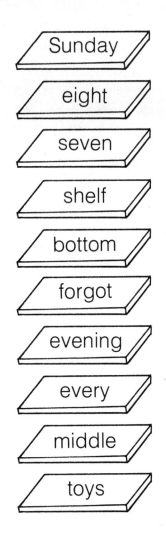

Sunday

eight

seven

shelf

bottom

forgot

evening

every

middle

toys

C **Put some things on the big shelf.**

1. Put a blue **X** on
   the middle shelf.

2. Put a brown ✔ on
   the bottom shelf.

3. Put a blue egg on
   the middle shelf.

4. Put a black box on
   the top shelf.

5. Put a red ▲ on
   every shelf.

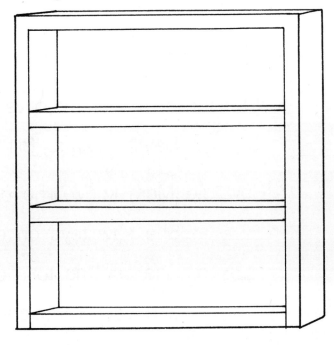

D **Circle one word that fits both sentences.**

too   top

1. A bird sat on ____ of the tree.

2. Bill played with his toy ____.

play   day

3. Mom and Dad went to see a ____.

4. Children like to run and ____.

can   care

5. The children must take ____ of the toys.

6. Bob did not ____ when Bev took his toy.

E **Look back at Story 6. Put the right child's name on each line.**

1. _____ was seven years old.

2. _____ was eight.

3. _____ was ten years old.

4. _____ had the top toy shelf.

5. _____ had the middle shelf.

6. _____ forgot to put away the toys.

Bev

Bill

Bob

Ducks like to be in water. They can swim fast. They play games in the water. They find food there, too. Ducks eat little bugs and fish. They pull plants out of the water to eat.

Ducks have big orange feet. The feet are good for pushing the water. Their feet make ducks good swimmers. Ducks' feet are not so good for walking and running. Their feet are not good for climbing.

Sometimes ducks must come out of the water. They can not walk as well as they can swim. Ducks must take care on land. If ducks are not careful on land, a fox may catch them.

Why do you think a fox likes to catch a duck?

A **Which one is right? Put a 🖌 by it.**

1. Why do foxes like to catch ducks?

_____ a. to make friends

_____ b. to play games

_____ c. for food

2. What do ducks like to eat?

_____ a. birds

_____ b. foxes

_____ c. bugs and plants

3. What can ducks use their feet to do?

_____ a. climb trees

_____ b. push water

_____ c. talk fast

4. Why don't foxes catch ducks in the water?

_____ a. Foxes don't swim well.

_____ b. Water is too cold.

_____ c. Ducks catch foxes.

5. Which animal is most like a duck?

_____ a. robin   _____ b. bee   _____ c. fox

6. What will you never see a duck do?

_____ a. climb a big tree

_____ b. eat in the water

_____ c. swim very fast

7. What is the best name for this story?

_____ a. How Ducks Climb

_____ b. How Ducks Catch Bugs

_____ c. Why Ducks Like Water

B What do you know about ducks?
Circle the right ones.

1. Which is the duck's foot?

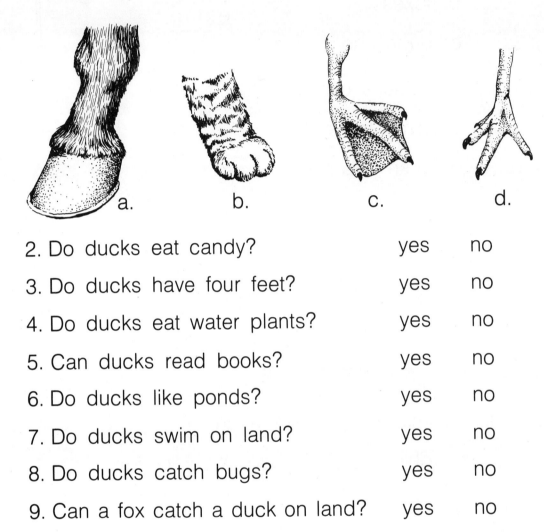

a.　　　　　b.　　　　　c.　　　　　d.

2. Do ducks eat candy?　　　　　　yes　　no

3. Do ducks have four feet?　　　　yes　　no

4. Do ducks eat water plants?　　　yes　　no

5. Can ducks read books?　　　　　yes　　no

6. Do ducks like ponds?　　　　　　yes　　no

7. Do ducks swim on land?　　　　　yes　　no

8. Do ducks catch bugs?　　　　　　yes　　no

9. Can a fox catch a duck on land?　yes　　no

C Can you guess the riddles? Circle the right word.

1. I am little.
   I have many feet.
   Ducks eat me.
   Children do not eat me.
   What am I?

2. I am an animal.
   I have four feet.
   Ducks must watch
   out for me.
   What am I?

bag　bug　bird　　　　bug　fox　bird

D Draw lines to match the opposites. One is done for you.

1. push
2. in
3. up
4. on
5. go
6. big
7. good

stop
down
pull
little
bad
here
off
out

E Look at a book's Table of Contents page. You can see the number of the page where each story starts. Can you answer these?

1. On which page can you find **Fish's Home?** _____

2. What story starts on page 8?

   _____
   _____

3. Is there a story about a turtle in this book?

   _____
   _____

Stories

Bug's Toy 2
Fish's Home 4
Lost Duck 5
Baby Monkey 7
Rabbit's House 8

One night a little yellow bird hopped around. She hopped around in the grass. She looked here and there. She was looking for something to eat. Soon the yellow bird saw a fat worm in the grass. She went to pick up the fat worm.

Just then, a tiger went by. The tiger hid in the tall grass. He looked at the little bird. When the bird pulled at the worm, the tiger jumped! He jumped at the yellow bird! He wanted to eat the bird.

But birds are quick. The little yellow bird got away! She flew far away. The tiger was left with the fat worm.

And tigers do not like to eat worms!

A **Which one is right? Put a** ✔ **by it.**

1. What is this story about?

_____ a. a tiger eating

_____ b. a fast bird

_____ c. what worms eat

2. What was the bird doing?

_____ a. looking for food

_____ b. sitting in a tree

_____ c. looking for a tiger

3. What was the tiger doing?

_____ a. eating worms

_____ b. flying away

_____ c. looking for food

4. Where was the bird?

_____ a. in a tree

_____ b. in a nest

_____ c. in the grass

5. When was the bird looking for food?

_____ a. in the morning

_____ b. in the afternoon

_____ c. at night

6. Who got some food in the story?

_____ a. no one

_____ b. the tiger

_____ c. the bird

7. What color was the bird?

_____ a. brown _____ b. yellow _____ c. blue

8. What do you think the worm did?

_____ a. ate the bird

_____ b. got away

_____ c. looked for a tiger

9. A **quick** tiger is a _____ tiger.

_____ a. pretty   _____ b. little   _____ c. fast

10. What is the best name for this story?

_____ a. The Tiger's Dinner

_____ b. How Worms Get Birds

_____ c. The Bird That Got Away

B **Read the words on the worms. Then read what to do. Can you mark the right words?**

tiger   worm   hopped   tall

hunt   left   green   quick

1. Make a ✔ on the word that means **jumped.**
2. Circle the name of the animal with four feet.
3. Put a box around the color of grass.
4. Put an **X** on the word that means **went away.**
5. Circle the word that means **big.**
6. Put a △ on the word that means **to look for.**
7. Put a line under the word that means **fast.**

C Put a ✔ by each one that is right about Story 8.

_____ 1. The tiger found some grass to eat.

_____ 2. The worm wanted to eat a fat tiger.

_____ 3. Tigers like to eat worms.

_____ 4. The bird pulled at the worm.

_____ 5. Birds like to eat worms.

_____ 6. The bird got away fast.

_____ 7. The bird picked up the tiger.

_____ 8. The worm was fat.

_____ 9. The tiger hid in the tall grass.

D What are Betty Bird and Will Worm doing? Put a ✔ by each sentence that tells what they are doing.

1. _____ a. Betty hunts for food.

_____ b. Betty hops into the water.

_____ c. Betty plays with a tiger.

2. _____ a. Will hid in a box.

_____ b. Will hid in the grass.

_____ c. Will hid in an apple.

3. _____ a. Betty Bird pulls on a worm.

_____ b. Will Worm pulls on a bird.

_____ c. The bird and worm play.

Last Monday, ten children had a race. The race was on the school playground.

Mr. Pack started the race. He told the children to stand side-by-side.

"Get ready. One! Two! Three! Go!" called Mr. Pack.

Away went the children. They ran faster and faster. Other children saw them run by.

"Hurry! Hurry! Run faster!" the other children called out.

Lupe fell down. Then he could not run again. Pam's shoe came off. She had to stop, too!

Mr. Pack called, "May wins the race!"

Jeff came in second, with Rita after him. Ted was last in the race.

A **How did they do in the race? Look at the story again. Write the names on the lines.**

first   second

1. _____   2. _____

next   last

3. _____   4. _____

40

B **Which one is right? Put a ✔ by it.**

1. What is this story about?

_____ a. Mr. Pack's playground

_____ b. a boat race

_____ c. children in a race

2. When was the race?

_____ a. last Monday

_____ b. last night

_____ c. last Sunday

3. Who watched the race?

_____ a. children _____ b. fathers _____ c. mothers

4. Why did Pam stop running?

_____ a. She fell.

_____ b. She saw her friend.

_____ c. Her shoe came off.

5. Who stopped running before the race was over?

_____ a. two girls

_____ b. a boy and a girl

_____ c. two boys

6. How many children ran to the end of the race?

_____ a. ten _____ b. nine _____ c. eight

7. Who came in before Rita?

_____ a. Jeff _____ b. Ted _____ c. Bob

8. Who won the race?

_____ a. Rita _____ b. Jeff _____ c. May

9. If you **hurry**, you are _____.

_____ a. sad _____ b. quick _____ c. happy

C Draw lines to match these.

1. to go very fast

2. It is on a foot.

3. a place to learn

4. after the first

5. looked at

6. made it begin

7. name of a day

8. set to go

9. at the end

10. a place to play

11. a game to see who
    can go fast

second

hurry

school

side

Monday

shoe

started

race

watched

last

playground

ready

D **Read each action word. When you put er on the action word, you name a person who does the action.**

1. help — helper   2. start — starter
3. run — runner   4. play — player
5. win — winner   6. jump — jumper

Circle the right word for each sentence.

1. Mr. Pack will _____ the race.

     start   starter

2. May was the _____ of the race.

     win   winner

3. There were ten _____ in the race.

     run   runners

4. Lupe fell and could not _____ again.

     run   runner

E **Fun Time! Can you do this?**

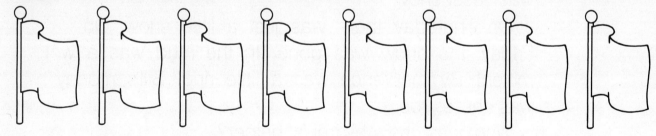

1. How many flags do you see? _____
2. Color the first one blue.
3. Color the last one yellow.
4. Color the second one green.
5. Circle the next to the last one.
6. Color the next to the last one brown.
7. Color four others red.

It snowed all day on Monday. On Tuesday Pat and Bill played in the white snow. They jumped and fell in it.

Bill lost one mitten and some money. Pat lost her ring in the deep, deep snow.

"I want my ring," said Pat. "Please help me find it, Mom!"

Mom said, "No, Pat. The snow is too deep."

"Where is my money?" asked Bill. "No one will help me find it."

Then Dad said, "Soon something big and yellow will help you find the lost things."

On Wednesday, the sun was in the sky. There was less snow.

On Thursday there was just a little snow. On Friday, the snow was gone. In the mud was a wet mitten! By the fence was a little ring. Bill's money was there, too.

Who was the children's helper?

A **Which one is right? Put a ✔ by it.**

1. When did the snow start to fall?

_____ a. Monday

_____ b. Wednesday

_____ c. Thursday

2. How do you think Bill's money got lost?

_____ a. Pat hid it in the snow.

_____ b. When Bill fell, the money dropped out.

_____ c. Someone took it out of his mitten.

3. Why didn't Pat find her ring?

_____ a. The trees hid it.

_____ b. Pat left it in her room.

_____ c. The snow was too deep.

4. Where was the ring?

_____ a. under the tree

_____ b. by the fence

_____ c. under the flowers

5. What came first in the story?

_____ a. A mitten was found.

_____ b. Pat asked Mom for help.

_____ c. They played in the snow.

6. Who was the children's helper?

_____ a. a truck _____ b. a moon _____ c. the sun

7. What is the best name for this story?

_____ a. Fun in the Mud

_____ b. The Sun and the Snow

_____ c. The Lost Fence

B **Draw lines to match these.**

1. not as many

2. something for hands

3. cannot be found

4. It falls from the sky.

5. the color of snow

6. day after Wednesday

7. a penny

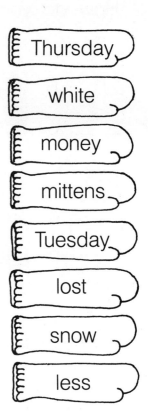

Thursday

white

money

mittens

Tuesday

lost

snow

less

C **Which one is right? Put a ✔ by it.**

1. Three of us came into the room. I came in first. Bill came in last. Pat was _____.

_____ a. the last one

_____ b. the first one

_____ c. the middle one

2. Pat and Bill wanted to go to the zoo on Monday. Mom and Dad had to work on Monday. Dad said they would all go to the zoo the next day. When will they go to the zoo?

_____ a. on Monday

_____ b. on Tuesday

_____ c. on Sunday

D **Write the days in order.**

Friday Wednesday Tuesday Monday Thursday

1. **Sunday**   2. _____

3. _____   4. _____

5. _____   6. _____

7. **Saturday**

E **Read each story. Circle the words that tell about the story.**

1. The sun is hot. It helps the trees get big. It melts the snow.

This story is about the _____.

a. trees   b. sun   c. flowers

2. On Monday, there was a lot of snow. The sun came out on Tuesday. On Wednesday, there was less snow. On Thursday, the snow was gone.

This story is about _____.

a. how the snow hid the cars

b. how deep the snow was

c. how the snow melted

3. Bill's cat was by the fence. The snow fell. The cat ran into the house. Pat had to dry the cat's feet.

This is a story about _____.

a. wet mittens   b. wet feet   c. wet money

A **Read this story.**

All the children are going to a show.
Bev is going to the show on Monday.
Lupe is going the day before Bev.
Jeff is going the day after Bev.
Rita is going the day before Sunday.
Pat is going the day after Tuesday.

When are they going to the show? Draw lines to
match each child to the right day.

1.  Pat

    a. Sunday

    b. Monday

2.  Rita

    c. Tuesday

3.  Bev

    d. Wednesday

4.  Lupe

    e. Thursday

    f. Friday

5.  Jeff

    g. Saturday

B Each shelf must have three words. Put the words below on the right shelves.

Colors

- - - - - - - -
- - - - - - - -
- - - - - - - -

Numbers

- - - - - - - -
- - - - - - - -
- - - - - - - -

Animals

- - - - - - - -
- - - - - - - -
- - - - - - - -

1. tiger
4. worm
7. duck
10. again

2. yellow
5. seven
8. green

3. eight
6. white
9. nine

C Draw lines to match these.

1. not as much

2. to look for

3. after the first

4. went away

5. late in the day

6. at the end

7. fast

8. all of them

snow

left

less

evening

hunt

second

every

quick

last

D **Can you guess the riddles? Circle the right word.**

1. I go up, up, up.
   I have grass on me.
   You can run up
   and down on me.
   What am I?

   hill   fox   water

2. I am white.
   I fall from the sky.
   I fall on cold days.
   Children play with me.
   What am I?

   sun   rain   snow

3. I am wet.
   Fish live in me.
   Children swim in me.
   Ducks sit on me.
   What am I?

   water   hill   box

4. I am a swimmer.
   I like the water.
   I have no feet.
   You like to catch me.
   What am I?

   fox   fish   duck

5. I am little.
   Birds try to get me.
   I have no feet.
   I stay in the grass.
   What am I?

   worm   fox   cat

6. I can run fast.
   I run after birds.
   I have four legs.
   I do not eat worms.
   What am I?

   bug   duck   tiger

E **Can you do this?**

1. Put an **X** on the middle book.

2. Color the top book green.

3. Color the bottom book orange.

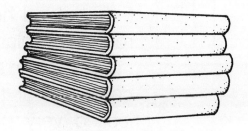

4. Make a hole in the bottom.

5. Color the hole brown.

6. Color the shoe yellow.

F **Circle the one word that fits both sentences.**

      last   left

1. Turn ____ at the corner.

2. The bird ____ in a hurry.

      last   left

3. I was ____ in line.

4. The race will ____ a long time.

G **Can you do this?**

1. Put an **X** on the page where **Jeff's Ring** starts.

2. Put a line under the story found on page 8.

3. On what page is **A Lost Puppy**? Write it here. ____

Stories

51

In the spring, Fay planted seeds in a window box. Pete helped her plant the seeds. They liked the color red. They planted all red flowers.

Little green plants came up first. Then red flowers came out of the green plants. The window box looked very pretty.

Two birds came to the window box. The birds had some seeds in their beaks. One bird dropped a seed. The seed fell into the window box. Fay and Pete did not see the birds.

One day, the children looked at their pretty red flowers. They saw a big purple flower with all the red flowers! What a surprise!

"How did the purple flower get there?" asked Pete.

"I do not know," said Fay. "We planted all red flowers."

They never found out how the purple flower got there. Do you know?

A Which one is right? Put a ✓ by it.

1. When did Fay plant seeds in the window box?

   _____ a. fall _____ b. winter _____ c. spring

2. What is this story about?

   _____ a. a big red flower

   _____ b. what birds eat

   _____ c. a purple surprise

3. What came out of the seeds first?

   _____ a. red flowers

   _____ b. green plants

   _____ c. brown birds

4. Why did the birds have seeds?

   _____ a. to plant them

   _____ b. to eat them

   _____ c. for gifts to the children

5. How did the purple flower get into the box?

   _____ a. Pete planted it there.

   _____ b. Fay put it there as a surprise.

   _____ c. A bird dropped a seed.

6. What is the best name for this story?

   _____ a. A Big Surprise

   _____ b. Pretty Colors

   _____ c. A Nest in the Window Box

B Draw lines to match these.

1. time of year

2. We look out of it.

3. at no time

4. saw where it was

5. a color

6. put seeds in the ground

7. something we did not
   know about

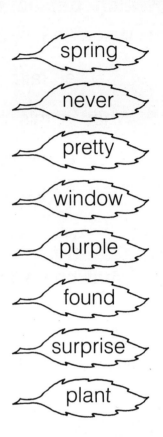

spring

never

pretty

window

purple

found

surprise

plant

C Circle the right word.

1. Little plants came
   | us |
   | up |
   .

2. Two birds
   | can |
   | came |
   to the window.

3. I saw a seed
   | drop |
   | chop |
   into the box.

4. How did the seed get
   | there |
   | they |
   ?

5. They
   | every |
   | never |
   did find out.

D **Read these sentences.**

1. How did the purple flower get here**?**
2. I did not plant purple flowers**.**

The first sentence **asks** something.
Use a **?** at the end.
The second sentence **tells** something.
Use a **.** at the end.

Put **?** or **.** at the end of each sentence.

1. Fay planted some seeds
2. Did Pete help plant seeds
3. Will little green plants come up first
4. Then flowers come out of the plants
5. A seed fell into the window box
6. Did a bird drop the seed

E **Find the sentence that means the same as the first one. Put a ✔ by it.**

1. They planted all red flowers.

_____ Every flower they planted was red.

_____ They planted one red flower.

2. Little green plants came up first.

_____ Little green plants came up after the flowers.

_____ Little green plants came up before the flowers.

3. The purple flower was a surprise.

_____ They planted the purple flower.

_____ They did not know the purple flower was there.

Mr. and Mrs. Hill had three children. Jay was ten years old. Kay was eight. Ray was six years old.

One afternoon, Ray came home from school. He had lost some of his things. He had lost his new book bag! He had lost his lunch box! And he had even lost all the buttons from his coat!

Mrs. Hill said, "Let's help Ray find his things."

The family hunted and looked. Jay found two buttons around the corner. Kay found one button in the dog house. Mrs. Hill found one button by the flowers. Mr. Hill saw the book bag under a tree. But they did not find the lunch box.

The next day, Ray went to school again. There was his lunch box by a window. Ray had left it there.

A **Which one is right? Put a ✔ by it.**

1. How old was Ray?

_____ a. seven _____ b. four _____ c. six

2. What is this story about?

_____ a. a lost girl

_____ b. two boys who lost things

_____ c. how the family helped Ray

3. How many buttons were on Ray's coat?

_____ a. four _____ b. three _____ c. two

4. Who found the lunch box?

_____ a. Kay _____ b. Ray _____ c. Jay

5. Who found two buttons?

_____ a. Kay _____ b. Ray _____ c. Jay

6. Who found the book bag?

_____ a. Mrs. Hill

_____ b. Mr. Hill

_____ c. Kay Hill

7. How did the book bag get under the tree?

_____ a. Kay put it there.

_____ b. Ray put it there and forgot it.

_____ c. The book bag walked there.

8. What must Ray learn to do?

_____ a. stay at home

_____ b. get a new coat

_____ c. take care of his things

B Where was each thing found? Draw lines to match them.

PLACES

1. around the corner

2. under a tree

3. by the flowers

4. in a hole

5. in a dog house

6. at school

THINGS

a.

b.

c.

d.

e.

C Find the sentence that means the same as the first one. Put a ✔ by it.

1. Mr. and Mrs. Hill had three children.

_____ They had three girls and one boy.

_____ They had one girl and two boys.

2. Ray left the school at noon.

_____ He went into the school at noon.

_____ He came out of the school at noon.

3. They lost the book again.

_____ They lost the book one more time.

_____ They never lost the book.

D Draw lines to match these.

1. two and one

2. a man

3. did not find

4. let us

5. noon meal

6. It is on a coat.

let's

Mr.

button

Mrs.

lost

three

lunch

E Put the words that tell **where** in the **WHERE?** box. Put the words that tell **when** in the **WHEN?** box. Draw lines to the right box. The first one is done for you.

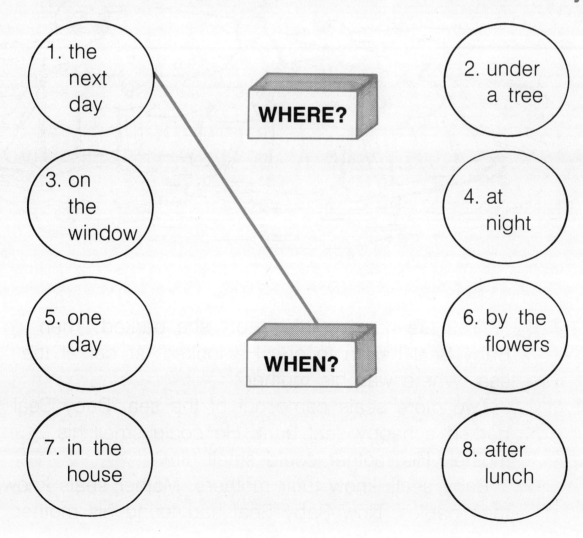

1. the next day

2. under a tree

WHERE?

3. on the window

4. at night

5. one day

WHEN?

6. by the flowers

7. in the house

8. after lunch

Baby Seal was asleep on a big rock. Mother Seal was gone. She went to look for food in the water.

Baby Seal got up and looked around. He saw many big mother seals. But he did not see his mother.

A mother seal came up out of the water. Baby Seal barked, "Mother!" He went over to her. The mother seal looked at him.

"You are not my little pup!" she barked. Then Baby Seal began to cry. He looked far out at the sea. Where was his mother?

Two more seals came out of the sea. Baby Seal barked a happy seal bark. He could smell his mother. His mother could smell him.

Baby seals know their mothers. Mother seals know their babies. Now Baby Seal had found his mother.

A Which one is right? Put a ✔ by it.

1. This story is about a seal

____ a. looking for its home.

____ b. looking for its mother.

____ c. looking for a hunter.

2. What are baby seals called?

____ a. pups ____ b. kids ____ c. kittens

3. What noise do seals make?

____ a. mew ____ b. bark ____ c. moo

4. Which one came first?

____ a. Baby Seal found his mother.

____ b. A seal said, "You are not my pup."

____ c. Baby Seal began to cry.

5. Why did Baby Seal cry?

____ a. He wanted to go to sleep.

____ b. He fell into the cold water.

____ c. He wanted to be with his mother.

6. How do mother seals know their babies?

____ a. by their smell

____ b. by their look

____ c. by their cry

B Draw lines to match these.

1. baby seal or dog

2. She takes care of her children.

3. something seals sit on

4. not here

5. a very little child

6. made a dog noise

7. move in the water

8. tell with your nose

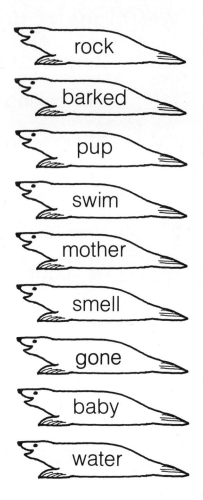

rock

barked

pup

swim

mother

smell

gone

baby

water

C Every sentence has a mark at the end that says "Stop!" A sentence that **asks** you something has **?** at the end. A sentence that **tells** you something has **.** at the end. Put **?** or **.** at the end of each sentence.

1. What did the seals find in the sea

2. Is the water cold

3. The seals barked

4. Is the rock too big to pick up

5. Seals can smell each other

6. Could they see any seals

7. Who began to cry

8. Did they eat many fish

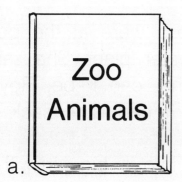 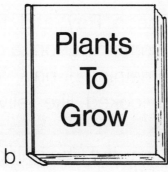 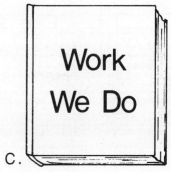

Zoo Animals

Plants To Grow

Work We Do

a.   b.   c.

D Look at the three books. Which book would you use to find out about each thing? Write a letter in each box. The first one is done for you.

b	1. flowers that grow fast
	2. how to put out fires
	3. animals that live in water
	4. tigers and monkeys
	5. little trees
	6. cleaning the streets
	7. building a house
	8. seeds of many kinds
	9. working on cars
	10. animals that can fly

One afternoon Roy and Rosa were at the pond. Rosa saw something on a water plant. She said, "Here is something funny. What can it be, Roy?"

The thing looked like jelly. It had little black spots in it.

The children put the thing into a big jar with water. They took it home. They watched it every day.

After six days, tadpoles came out of the eggs. They had long tails.

Soon back legs began to come out. The tails got shorter.

Then front legs began to come out. The tails got even shorter.

All four legs got big. The tails were gone!

Rosa said, "Now I know. I found frog eggs. Tadpoles came out of the eggs. Tadpoles are baby frogs!"

A **Which one is right? Put a ✓ by it.**

1. Who found something?

_____ a. a girl   _____ b. a boy   _____ c. a frog

2. Where did they see something funny?

     _____ a. in the water

     _____ b. in the sand

     _____ c. on a shelf

3. What is a tadpole?

     _____ a. a baby fish

     _____ b. a little duck

     _____ c. a little frog

4. What looked like jelly?

     _____ a. tadpoles   _____ b. frogs   _____ c. eggs

5. What came out first?

     _____ a. front legs   _____ b. back legs   _____ c. boots

6. What happened to the tadpole?

     _____ a. Its tail got very big.

     _____ b. It became an egg.

     _____ c. It became a frog.

7. What is the best name for this story?

     _____ a. What the Frog Found

     _____ b. What Rosa Found

     _____ c. A Bad Frog

B Draw lines to match these.

1. something to hold water

2. the opposite of back

3. something to walk on

4. something on the back of animals

5. not as long

6. something to eat on bread

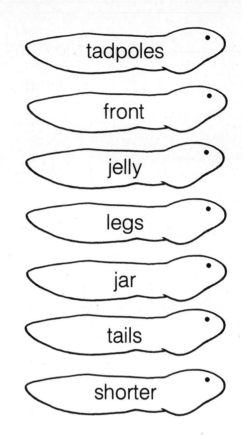

tadpoles

front

jelly

legs

jar

tails

shorter

C WHEN? WHERE? Go for a walk with the children. Put a ✔ on the ones that tell when. Put an **X** on the ones that tell where.

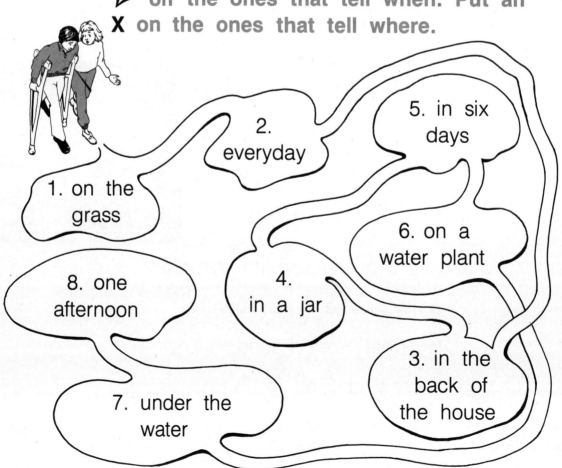

2. everyday

5. in six days

1. on the grass

6. on a water plant

8. one afternoon

4. in a jar

3. in the back of the house

7. under the water

D **Fun time! Read the sentence. Finish it. Circle the right picture.**

1. Roy put the funny thing in a _____.

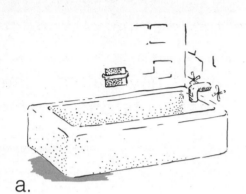
a.

b.

c.

2. They found eggs in the _____.

a.

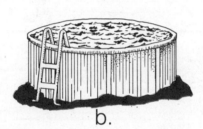
b.

c.

3. A front door is found on a _____.

a.

b.

c.

4. Roy and Rosa found something that looks like _____.

a.

b.

c.

67

One afternoon, a mother fox was out looking for food. Her two little foxes were with her. They saw some ducks in the pond.

Fred Fox said, "I like to eat duck. I wish we could catch one."

Mother Fox said, "We can't catch ducks in the water. They can swim too fast."

The foxes hid in the tall grass. They watched the ducks playing in the pond. At last, eight ducks came out on the land.

Mother Fox said, "Now we can catch a duck. Ducks don't walk fast."

"I'll grab that first duck," said Fran Fox.

"I'll grab that last duck," said Fred Fox.

Mother Fox said, "Wait until they get near us. Ready? Go!" The foxes jumped out of the grass.

As quick as can be, the ducks got away. Did they run away? No! Did they swim away? No! The ducks flew away!

Mother Fox said, "I forgot that ducks have wings. Now we have nothing to eat!"

A Which one is right? Put a ✓ by it.

1. Which one happened first?

_____ a. The foxes jumped at the ducks.

_____ b. The ducks came out of the water.

_____ c. The ducks got away.

2. Where did the ducks play?

_____ a. in the pond

_____ b. in the barn

_____ c. in the yard

3. Why did the foxes wait before jumping?

_____ a. They wanted to surprise the ducks.

_____ b. They wanted some help.

_____ c. They wanted Mother Fox to rest.

4. How did the ducks get away?

_____ a. by walking fast

_____ b. by jumping in the pond

_____ c. by flying away

5. What helps a duck fly?

_____ a. feet _____ b. water _____ c. wings

6. What is the best name for this story?

_____ a. A Good Dinner for the Foxes

_____ b. No Dinner for the Foxes

_____ c. Fred Fox Gets a Duck

B Draw lines to match these.

1. not far

2. take away fast

3. not any

4. water to swim in

5. animals

6. to want

7. up to the time of

8. They help birds fly.

9. ground

nothing

pond

near

last

grab

foxes

until

wish

land

wings

C A sentence that tells something ends with ..
A sentence that asks something ends with **?**.
Put . or **?** at the end of each sentence.

1. Are you ready to catch a duck

2. The foxes hid in the grass

3. The ducks played in the pond

4. Can foxes catch ducks in the water

5. Did the ducks run away

6. The ducks did not swim away

7. Do ducks have wings

8. Why did the ducks fly away

9. How many ducks did the foxes grab

D **Find the sentence that means the same as the first one. Put a ✔ by it.**

1. They were by a pond.

_____ a. They were near a fence.

_____ b. They were near the water.

_____ c. They were near the tall grass.

2. Fran walked last.

_____ a. Fran was in the middle.

_____ b. Fran was in back.

_____ c. Fran was first.

E **Find the sentence that goes with each picture. Put the right letter under the picture.**

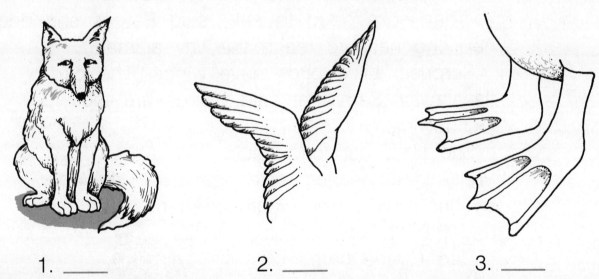

1. _____   2. _____   3. _____

a. A duck's feet can push the water.
b. Birds use them to fly.
c. This animal likes to eat ducks.
d. The ducks fly over the pond.

One afternoon Mrs. Giraffe went to the water hole. She went to get a drink. Baby Giraffe did not want to go with her mother.

Mrs. Giraffe said, "Stay here Baby Pat and do not go away."

Soon Pat wanted something good to eat. She forgot what her mom told her.

She walked into the tall grass. She saw a fat worm.

Pat wanted to eat the worm. But Pat was too tall. The worm crawled away.

Next Pat saw a little bird on a nest.

"That looks good to eat," said Pat as she bent her long neck to reach the tiny animal.

Surprise! Little birds have wings. The bird flew away. Baby Pat said, "Birds are too fast for me."

She lifted her long neck. Pretty green leaves were right by her mouth. Her mouth opened and Pat ate the leaves.

Dad Giraffe came by. "Good for you!" he said. "You have found the best food for giraffes. You found it by yourself."

A **Which one is right? Put a ✔ by it.**

1. Which one happened first?

_____ a. The worm crawls away.

_____ b. The giraffe sees a worm.

_____ c. The giraffe eats some leaves.

2. Where did Mom Giraffe go?

_____ a. to the water hole

_____ b. to the big tree

_____ c. to see the bird in the nest

3. Why are leaves the best food for giraffes to eat?

_____ a. The leaves are pretty and are by the water hole.

_____ b. Long necks help giraffes reach leaves on tall trees.

_____ c. Giraffes can reach down to little animals under the grass.

4. What words tell about giraffes?

_____ a. long necks, long legs, wings

_____ b. short back legs, short tail, long fat neck

_____ c. long legs, long neck, spots on fur

5. What is the best name for this story?

_____ a. Dad at the Water Hole

_____ b. A Giraffe Helps Herself

_____ c. Mom Giraffe Finds a Drink

B Draw lines to match these.

1. to get up to something

2. very little

3. where to put food

4. to take away fast

5. to move on hands and feet

6. picked up

7. look at something
   for a long time

8. They help birds fly.

9. It is under your head.

10. It is what we do with milk.

grab

drink

neck

crawl

bent

watch

reach

tiny

lifted

mouth

wings

C Do the animals eat plants or meat? If they eat other animals they are meat eaters.
Write **plants** next to the plant eaters.
Write **meat** next to the meat eaters.

1. _____

2. _____

3. _____

4. _____

D Find the sentence that means the same as the first one. Put a ✔ by it.

1. Ray can reach the shelf.

_____ a. He can play with it.

_____ b. He can get to it.

_____ c. He can not get to it.

2. Baby Giraffe walked in front of the others.

_____ a. She was in the middle.

_____ b. She was the first.

_____ c. She was in back.

3. They lifted a frog.

_____ a. They saw an animal.

_____ b. They picked up an animal.

_____ c. They put down an animal.

E Put a ✔ by the words that tell **where.**
Put an **X** by the words that tell **when.**

1. _____ that evening

2. _____ into her pouch

3. _____ before dinner

4. _____ on the leaves

5. _____ on the grass

6. _____ after school

7. _____ all day

8. _____ under the nest

SKILLS REVIEW (Stories 11–16)

A Four leaves are on each tree. Put the
number of each word on the right tree.
The first one is done for you.

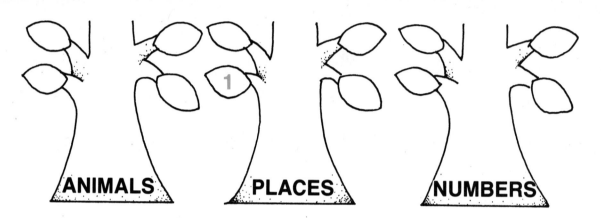

ANIMALS   PLACES   NUMBERS

1. sea	2. kangaroo	3. pond
4. giraffe	5. five	6. eight
7. six	8. seal	9. school
10. ten	11. bird	12. dog house

B Draw lines to match these.

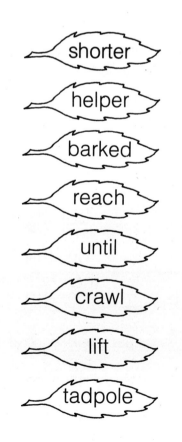

1. to pick up

2. to get to it

3. not as long

4. one who works with you

5. up to the time of

6. made a dog noise

7. a baby frog

shorter

helper

barked

reach

until

crawl

lift

tadpole

C **What do you know about foxes and seals?**

1. Circle the fox's nose.

2. Put a ✔ on the seal's nose.

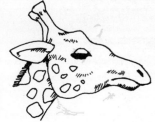   

D **Circle yes or no.**

1. Does a kangaroo have two ears?	yes	no
2. Can a tadpole push a car?	yes	no
3. Will a fox eat a bird?	yes	no
4. Do giraffes have wings?	yes	no
5. Do giraffes have long necks?	yes	no
6. Will a seal eat a fish?	yes	no
7. Can a seal fly?	yes	no
8. Do tadpoles have tails?	yes	no
9. Can a seal swim?	yes	no
10. Do seals read fast?	yes	no

E **Put ? or . at the end of each sentence.**

1. How did the purple flower get there

2. What hopped on two big back feet

3. Are the front legs shorter

4. Ray found his lunch box at school

5. Did the seals eat many fish

6. Baby Seal could smell his mother

7. The giraffe reaches leaves with its long neck

77

F Can you do this?

1. Color six flowers purple.
   Color the other one red.

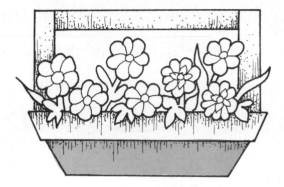

2. Here is Ray's coat.
   Put four green buttons
   on it.

3. Sara and Dad worked
   until five o'clock.
   Show this time on
   the clock.

4. Here is what Rosa saw.
   Put an **X** on what came
   out of the eggs. Circle
   the mother animal.

5. Mother Fox and her
   little foxes are
   looking for food.
   Color the two little
   foxes brown. Color
   Mother Fox red.

G Find the sentence that means the same as the first one. Put a ✔ by it.

1. We hunted for the toy.

_____ a. We played with the toy.

_____ b. We looked for the toy.

2. Rosa is shorter than Roy.

_____ a. Rosa is not as tall as Roy.

_____ b. Rosa is bigger than Roy.

3. The worm crawled to the rock.

_____ a. The worm reached the rock.

_____ b. The worm dropped the rock.

H WHEN? WHERE? Put the words that tell **when** in the **WHEN?** box. Put the words that tell **where** in the **WHERE?** box. Draw lines to the right box.

1. at school

2. in the pond

3. long ago

WHEN?

4. in the spring

5. now

6. on the sofa

7. one day

8. next to me

9. after lunch

WHERE?

10. by the sea

I Circle the right word.

1. Mother Seal went back to the rock.
She wanted to _____ for her baby.

   car   care   can

2. Mother frogs lay eggs. Then they go away.
They _____ see the tadpoles come out.

   ever   every   never

3. Mother came in and found a _____. Black spots were on the sofa. Mother saw the cat's feet. She knew where the spots came from.

   surprise   nothing   something

J Can you do this?

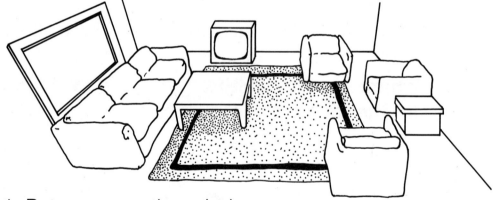

1. Put a ✔ on the window.
2. Put a blue book on the big table.
3. Write how many chairs you see. _____
4. Color the rug purple.
5. Put a green plant on the little table.
6. Color the sofa brown.
7. Color the TV black.
8. Put a red button next to the book on the big table.